	DATE DUE		

Science
and
Sustainable Wildlife Habitats

Peggy J. Parks

San Diego, CA

ReferencePoint Press®

© 2018 ReferencePoint Press, Inc.
Printed in the United States

For more information, contact:
ReferencePoint Press, Inc.
PO Box 27779
San Diego, CA 92198
www.ReferencePointPress.com

LIBRARY OF CONGRESS CATALOGING-IN-PUBLICATION DATA

Name: Parks, Peggy J., 1951– author.
Title: Science and Sustainable Wildlife Habitats/by Peggy J. Parks.
Description: San Diego, CA: ReferencePoint Press, Inc., 2018. | Series: Science and Sustainability | Audience: Grade 9 to 12. | Includes bibliographical references.
Identifiers: LCCN 2017028354 (print) | LCCN 2017029287 (ebook) | ISBN 9781682822609 (eBook) | ISBN 9781682822593 (hardback)
Subjects: LCSH: Wildlife conservation—Juvenile literature. | Habitat (Ecology)—Juvenile literature. | Sustainable development—Juvenile literature. | Wildlife resources—Climatic factors.
Classification: LCC QL83 (ebook) | LCC QL83 .P3735 2018 (print) | DDC 333.95/416--dc23
LC record available at https://lccn.loc.gov/2017028354

CONTENTS

INTRODUCTION

Saving Habitats to Save Wildlife

"We are losing species and their habitats at an alarming rate."

—US Fish and Wildlife Service

US Fish and Wildlife Service, "Strategic Habitat Conservation FAQs," January 21, 2016. www.fws.gov.

A habitat is a place where animals, birds, fish, and plants live or grow in a natural state. For wildlife, habitats are where they can find enough food and water to survive, take refuge from predators and hostile conditions, and have ample space to raise their young. These habitats are found all over the world, from prairies, tropical rain forests, and mountain ranges to oceans, freshwater lakes, wetlands, and rivers. One ocean habitat that scientists find especially fascinating is at the National Marine Sanctuary in Monterey Bay, California. A giant kelp forest located there is one of the most diverse wildlife habitats in the world.

Kelp is a type of brown seaweed with long, tough stalks. Following shorelines, mostly along the rocky Pacific coast, kelp grows tall and thick, forming massive underwater forests. The kelp forest at Monterey Bay is populated by hundreds of species of marine wildlife, including jellyfish, sea stars, snails, crabs, and sea urchins, as well as sea lions, seals, and sea otters. Of all the marine creatures that live in the Monterey Bay kelp forest, the sea otters do the most to keep the ecological system, or ecosystem, in balance. Sea otters live in kelp forests to take refuge from severe storms and also to hide from sharks. The otters feed on sea urchins and other marine invertebrates (creatures without backbones, such as sea stars, crabs, and jellyfish) that graze on giant kelp. Invertebrates eat massive quantities of kelp and can destroy an entire forest if left to multiply unchecked. By feeding on sea urchins, sea otters help keep the population of these creatures under control. As a result, the kelp forest continues to grow and thrive, providing a habitat for the rich diversity of wildlife species that depend on it for survival.

Habitat Loss

No matter where habitats are located, the greatest threat to them is human actions: pollution, the leveling of forests for farmland, cutting up land for development and road building, filling in wetlands, and global warming. These actions have damaged or destroyed many of earth's wildlife habitats, which endangers wildlife and puts species at risk for extinction. "Every day there are fewer places left that wildlife can call home,"[1] says the National Wildlife Federation.

Wildlife scientists categorize habitat loss as one of three major types: destruction, fragmentation, and degradation. Some ways habitats are destroyed include harvesting fossil fuels such as coal, clear-cutting forests, and filling in wetlands. Habitat fragmentation occurs when habitats are cut up into fragments for road building or residential or industrial development. Marine wildlife can also lose habitats through fragmentation, such as when dams are built or water is diverted in other ways. Equally hazardous is habitat degradation, which is most commonly caused by pollution from untreated sewage, mining waste, fertilizers, and pesticides, among other substances.

According to the World Wildlife Fund (WWF) *Living Planet Report 2016*, earth's population of wild vertebrates (mammals, birds, reptiles, amphibians, and fish) declined 58 percent from

1970 to 2012. "In other words," the report authors write, "the total number of wild animals with backbones has fallen by more than half within one human lifetime."[2] The report also states that the number one cause of wildlife decline is habitat loss, especially due to unsustainable agriculture practices and logging. Habitat degradation is also playing a major role in the decline of wildlife populations.

Humans Undoing the Damage They Cause

Habitat loss poses a serious threat to wildlife throughout the world. But in the United States, the Endangered Species Act (ESA) does a great deal to protect wildlife. This legislation has been in effect since 1973, when the US Congress enacted the ESA to strengthen existing federal protections for wildlife. Under this law, for a species to be protected, it must be listed as threatened, meaning likely to become endangered soon; or endangered, which means on the brink of extinction now. The three key elements of the ESA are preventing listed species from being killed or harmed, protecting habitat essential for those species' survival, and creating plans to restore healthy populations of listed species.

Since the ESA has been in effect, it has meant the difference between survival and extinction for hundreds of America's wildlife species. One creature that was saved from extinction is the bald eagle. The majestic birds were nearly wiped out by a variety of human actions, including habitat destruction and contamination of food sources by the deadly pesticide DDT. When female eagles ate the poisoned food, it thinned the shells of their eggs, making them break easily, thus, killing their chicks. Although eagles had been under federal protection since 1967, the prolific use of DDT remained a deadly threat to them. In 1972, the year before the ESA became law, DDT was banned.

Once the ESA went into effect, bald eagle habitats (nesting areas) were protected more than they had ever been before. Captive

Threatened Animal Species, 2017

The International Union for Conservation of Nature (IUCN) every year surveys thousands of animal and plant species to monitor the status of the planet's biodiversity. Using these surveys the organization has identified certain trends. For example, between 1980 and 2012 coral species moved more rapidly toward extinction than any other species. And amphibians, on average during that same period, had the most threatened species. The threat status of species is generally categorized in one of three ways: critically endangered, endangered, and vulnerable. The IUCN statistics for six classes of animals reveal that in 2017 amphibians represented the largest critically endangered and endangered class, and fish represented the largest vulnerable class. While there are many reasons species struggle, habitat loss may represent the biggest threat of all.

Vulnerable		Endangered		Critically Endangered	
Group	2017	Group	2017	Group	2017
Mammals	527	Mammals	464	Mammals	203
Birds	787	Birds	448	Birds	225
Reptiles	426	Reptiles	424	Reptiles	240
Amphibians	670	Amphibians	852	Amphibians	545
Fish	1,238	Fish	660	Fish	461
Insects	653	Insects	419	Insects	226

Source: IUCN, "The IUCN Red List of Threatened Species," 2017. www.iucnredlist.org.

breeding programs were implemented, in which wildlife breeding took place in controlled environments such as wildlife reserves or zoos. When eagle chicks hatched and were deemed old enough to survive on their own, they were released into the wild. Thanks to these and other measures, the population of bald eagles has soared. According to the National Wildlife Federation, more than seven thousand breeding pairs live throughout the United States today—a startling increase from just four hundred breeding pairs in the late 1960s.

Numerous other wildlife species have also been saved by the ESA, including the Florida panther, humpback whale, grizzly bear,

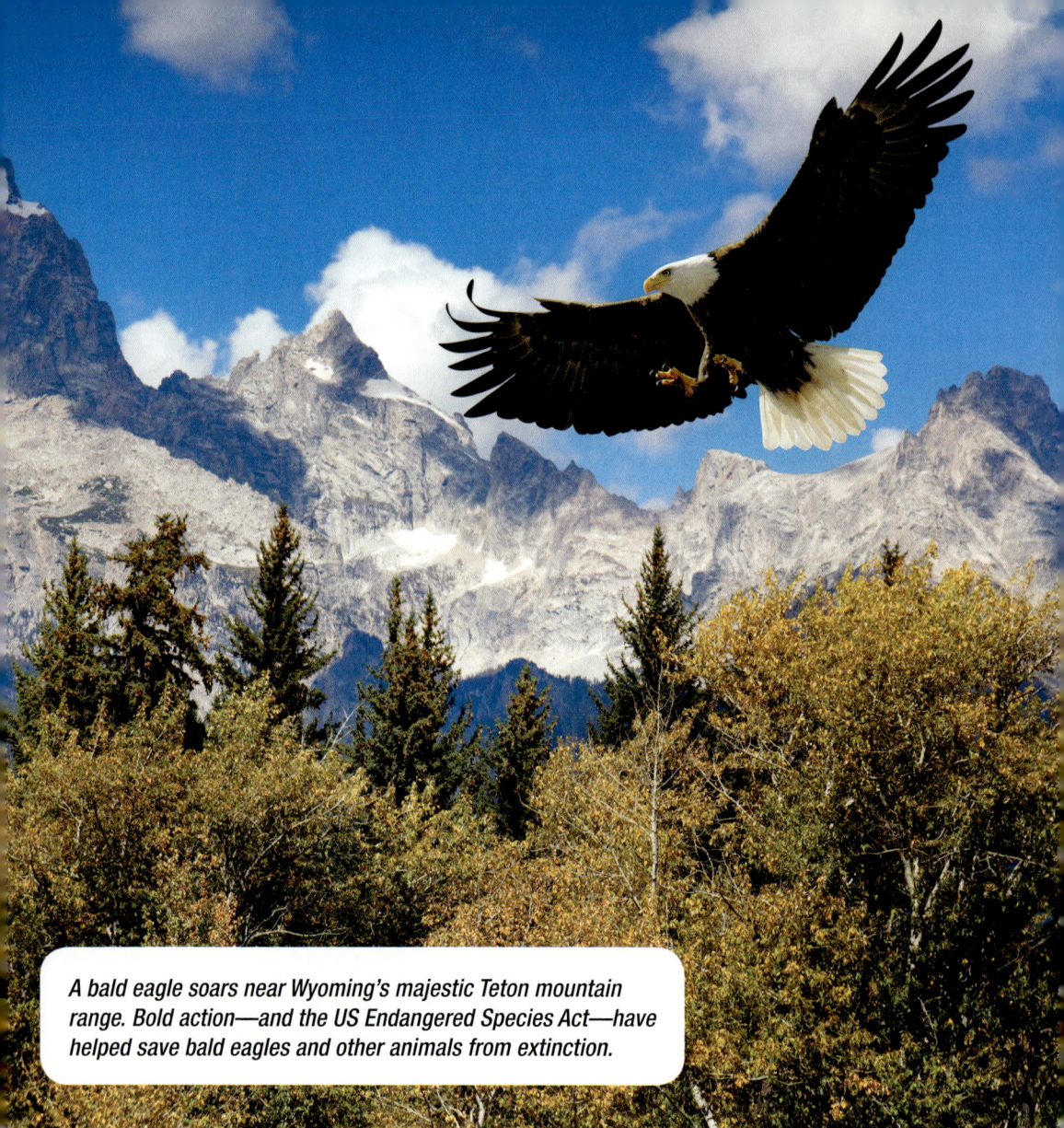

A bald eagle soars near Wyoming's majestic Teton mountain range. Bold action—and the US Endangered Species Act—have helped save bald eagles and other animals from extinction.

peregrine falcon, California condor, Florida manatee, gray wolf, black-footed ferret, and American alligator, among others. Between 1973 and 2013 the ESA prevented the extinction of 99 percent of the species that were under its protection. Equally important, says the Endangered Species Coalition, "millions of acres of forests, beaches, and wetlands—those species' essential habitats—have been protected from degradation."[3] Scientists throughout the world have praised the ESA as the standard by which other wildlife protection efforts should be measured.

Wildlife Protection Goes High-Tech

In recent years, as technology has grown more sophisticated, scientists have discovered innovative ways to protect wildlife and their habitats. New methods of tracking help monitor the behavior of wildlife while they are on the move. Sophisticated computer modeling software can depict what habitats looked like before humans degraded or destroyed them. High-tech cameras allow scientists to observe wildlife in ways never before possible. Even drones have proved to be invaluable tools for studying wildlife, as scientists can use them to photograph and videotape animals in their native habitats.

Despite the progress that has been made in protecting wildlife, challenges still abound. Habitats worldwide are being degraded and destroyed at a rapid rate, and wildlife species are suffering because of it. Many of these species risk extinction because of habitat loss. Yet scientists remain steadfast in their commitment to the study of wildlife and their habitats and to finding ways to undo the damage that humans have inflicted on habitats worldwide.

CHAPTER ONE

Science to the Rescue

> **"Science is at the core of wildlife conservation. It allows us to understand how to conserve wildlife and wild places and measure the impact of our work to save them."**
>
> —Cristian Samper, president of the Wildlife Conservation Society
>
> Quoted in Wildlife Conservation Society, "Science Is Core to Saving Wildlife," April 19, 2017. https://newsroom.wcs.org.

Habitat loss poses the single greatest threat to wildlife throughout the world. This widespread loss has already pushed numerous species to the brink of extinction. As the world's human population continues to increase, threats to habitats will likely grow. A larger population means more land is needed for agriculture, roads, housing, energy, and other types of development—meaning that ample space for wildlife to live and thrive will shrink even further. "Without a strong plan to create terrestrial and marine protected areas," says the WWF, "ecological habitats will continue to be lost."[4] That "strong plan" is where science comes into play.

The reason so much is known about habitat loss is because of technology. Scientists use a variety of techniques to survey and track wildlife, from sophisticated computer programs to high-tech photo equipment that can record and photograph animals in their natural habitats. Scientists use these innovative tools to learn more about wildlife, as well as learn how to better protect and preserve habitat. Scientific research, for instance, has led to more sustainable methods of farming, which saves land and preserves habitat. Better growing techniques help farmers in tropical countries grow crops without having to destroy forests. Advanced planning enables road building and other types of development to proceed without destroying habitat. Although all habitat cannot be saved, the efforts of scientists are helping conserve habitat throughout the world.

Exploring from Above

In recent years scientists have used unmanned aerial vehicles, more commonly known as drones, to study wildlife. Among the first to do this were conservation scientists Lian Pin Koh and Serge Wich, who are experts on orangutans. These great apes are the largest tree-dwelling, or arboreal, animals in the world. They live in the thick, dense rain forests of the Southeast Asian islands of Borneo and Sumatra. Orangutans spend nearly all their time swinging from tree to tree in the jungle and building nests in the treetops where they sleep. Scientific research about orangutans is critical because the creatures are threatened with extinction. Legal and illegal destruction of forests have devastated orangutan habitats. An estimated 80 percent of the world's orangutan population has disappeared over the past seventy-five years, and if drastic steps are not taken, these apes may become extinct.

> **WORDS IN CONTEXT**
>
> **arboreal**
>
> Relating to trees (often in reference to animals).

Koh and Wich have studied orangutans for many years and have spent a great deal of time in Sumatra. A primary focus of their research is to find out what is happening to the apes' habitats. If illegal logging is the problem, and they are able to find proof of that, they can alert the authorities. Their research can be challenging because orangutans build their nests so high in the trees—up to 65 feet (20 m) off the ground. To overcome this difficulty, the two scientists devised a plan in 2012 to explore the orangutan habitat from above using a drone. As it flew over the rain forest, an attached camera would capture photographs of orangutans and their treetop nests. Koh and Wich knew that

Researchers have had difficulty studying orangutan behavior because these apes spend a lot of time in dense jungle treetops. Camera-equipped drones provide a way to see orangutans in their natural habitats in Sumatra and in Borneo (pictured).

by using a drone they could get much closer to the trees than was possible with an airplane or helicopter. Convinced they had found the ideal solution to their research challenge, they built the drone themselves, outfitted it with a camera, and then prepared to launch it.

Exploring Treetop Habitats

Their first drone mission took place in February 2012. Once the drone was in the sky, Koh and Wich had no idea what to expect. "It was particularly nerve wracking," says Koh, "because we were not certain that the drone would return to us after that mission."[5]

It did return, however. And even though the camera produced only blurred images of orangutan nests, Koh and Wich were enthusiastic about their first drone mission. They believed the blurry photos were merely an indication that adjustments were needed to compensate for the vibration of the drone's motors. Convinced that they could fix these bugs, they left Sumatra and made plans for another drone mission later in the year.

In September 2012 Koh and Wich returned to the jungle for their second drone launch. Standing in the scorching Sumatran sun, they let the drone go and watched it fly away. "At the flick of a switch on the radio transmitter and a gentle toss," they write, "the Conservation Drone took off into the wind."[6] About ten minutes later they spotted the drone in the distance flying back toward them. When it landed, they carried it to their campsite and began downloading the camera's images to a laptop computer.

The pictures showed the tops of the rain forest canopy in vivid detail. And what Koh and Wich saw in those photos were broken and bent branches in the treetops, which they knew were characteristic of an orangutan nest. "And then we spotted another nest, and yet another,"[7] they write. Finally they had crisp, clear photos of orangutan nests, which they never had before. Motivated by what they had achieved with drones, the duo went on to found a group called Conservation Drones at the University of Adelaide in Australia. The group promotes the use of drone technology in wildlife research, particularly in developing countries where human-induced habitat loss is such an urgent problem.

Surveying Habitats from Above

The use of drones to study wildlife habitats has grown significantly in the years since Koh and Wich launched their first missions in Sumatra. Scientists throughout the world are discovering the advantages of using drones for all kinds of research. One scientist who is especially enthusiastic about the many possibilities of drones is David Bird, a wildlife biologist from Montreal, Canada. "I feel like a pioneer who's on the crest of a wave with groundbreaking technology,"[8] says Bird, who has used drones to study seabirds and their habitats.

In 2016 the conservation charity Fauna & Flora International launched a drone mission in the Koh Rong Archipelago, which is a string of islands off the coast of Cambodia. Photography captured during the drone mission clearly showed a sea grass habitat that had never before been charted. Sea grasses are flowering aquatic plants that can form thick, dense underwater meadows. These meadows serve as shallow water habitats and feeding grounds for a wide and diverse variety of species, including sea horses, sea turtles, marine mammals known as dugongs, numerous types of fish, and countless others.

Seagrass habitats are threatened by a number of human actions, including destructive fishing methods, unsustainable development, and pollution. Fauna & Flora researchers plan to use the photographs collected by drones to create habitat maps and identify areas that need more research and ultimately greater protection. "They will help us to conserve and monitor important habitats such as coral reefs, seagrass, and mangroves," says Nhem Vanna of the Cambodian Fisheries Administration. "This new technology will save us time while allowing us to conduct new research in Cambodia."[9]

Far away from Cambodia, another country where scientists are using drones for research is Mexico, which is a winter home for monarch butterflies. Every winter, tens of millions of butterflies migrate there from Canada and the United States. The monarchs take shelter in fir and pine trees, such as those at the Monarch Butterfly Biosphere Reserve in Michoacán, Mexico. These treetop habitats are critical to the butterflies' survival, which appears bleaker each year. Scientists who study monarch butterflies say that their population has declined more than 90 percent in the past several decades. They are threatened with extinction—and that is why a 2015 discovery made by drone photography was especially disturbing to wildlife scientists.

In flying over the reserve, the drone captured images of widespread deforestation. Researchers who examined the photos found that approximately 25 acres (10 ha) of trees vital to monarch butterfly survival had been illegally cut down in just one year. Although the felled trees were located outside the primary monarch wintering area, the logging almost completely wiped out a section known as the buffer zone. This area helps maintain the climate that is suitable for the butterflies' survival, protecting them from the extreme heat during the daytime and cold temperatures at night. Noted monarch researcher Lincoln Brower, who has studied monarch butterflies in Michoacán since 1977, called the loss of habitat "a catastrophe."[10] Although Brower was aware that illegal logging was taking place at the reserve, he had no idea how bad the problem was until he saw the drone photos. He hopes that officials from the reserve will take measures to stop the deforestation before the monarch population is gone forever.

THE DOWNSIDE OF LIVE FEEDS

High-tech photography involving webcams has been invaluable to wildlife research. While sitting at their computers, scientists can spot and monitor troubling activity or changes without disturbing wildlife. The ability to live stream those images has also proved to be of great interest to the public. People can log on to the websites of national parks or wildlife organizations and watch wildlife in action. This has one downside, however: Nature is not always kind. In fact, to humans nature can seem cruel at times. And some people who witness nature's cruelty become very disturbed by it.

This was shown to be true in 2014 when wildlife enthusiasts were watching an osprey family near the Massachusetts seashore. A Woods Hole Oceanographic Institution webcam was trained on the nest. Viewers had seen the mother laying eggs, incubating the eggs, and helping the chicks hatch. Then the mother began to neglect and attack her chicks, and people became agitated, with some demanding that the institution intervene and save the chicks. After the same thing happened in 2015 and the comments became threatening, Woods Hole took down the webcam. On its website was a short explanation: "Regrettably, the cam will not be operating this season due to the increasingly aggressive actions of certain viewers the last two years."

Quoted in Karin Bruilliard, "People Love Watching Nature on Nest Cams—Until It Gets Grisly," *Washington Post*, May 19, 2016. www.washingtonpost.com.

Artificial Intelligence

The problems caused by deforestation are also being revealed through sophisticated computer technology. One example is Terra-i, an artificial intelligence program that is helping scientists monitor forest loss (and therefore habitat loss) in a number of Latin American countries. Terra-i was developed by Andy Jarvis, a scientist with the International Centre for Tropical Agriculture. His work was inspired by a basic fact of nature: Green grass gets greener when it rains and turns brown when there is no rain. Based on that simple and logical fact, Jarvis created Terra-i, which has the unique ability to "learn" as it analyzes. This is possible because of its neural network, which Jarvis designed to mimic the human nervous system.

As Terra-i analyzes data, it learns which levels of greenness are associated with various amounts of rainfall during the year. When abnormal changes in greenness are detected, Terra-i flags them as potential problem areas. According to scientist Jerry Touval, who is based in Latin America, Terra-i is like an "early warning system" for habitats. "With one tool we can see where we're losing habitat, analyze the drivers of that loss, and determine where we should be working next,"[11] says Touval.

Terra-i has proved to be a remarkable scientific tool for monitoring habitat loss. Two of its findings are an average annual deforestation rate of 6.4 million acres (2.6 million ha) per year in Amazon rain forests and the loss of approximately 54 million acres (22 million ha) of other forested areas in Latin America. Because of these and other startling revelations about habitat loss, government officials in some Latin American countries are reviewing their conservation policies for possible changes. For example, Terra-i detected strange deforestation patterns in 2008 and 2009 along the Amazonian side of Caquetá in Colombia. Scientists following up on the discovery learned that the country's deforestation rate had doubled in five years, which shocked Colombian officials. "The Colombian government wasn't truly aware of the problem," says Nature Conservancy scientist Jose Yunis. "Essentially, Terra-i was the first to start seeing this."[12]

Illegal logging has resulted in deforestation in Colombia (pictured). Some scientists are using an artificial intelligence program that helps them identify forests that are being lost to illegal logging and other activities.

Computer Modeling

Technology like Terra-i is enabling scientists throughout the world to vastly expand their knowledge about wildlife and what must be done to protect animals and their habitats. Another example of such technology is a sophisticated computer program called LANDFIRE. Developed by scientists at the Nature Conservancy, LANDFIRE is a computer modeling program. It can help scientists understand the condition of natural habitats long ago—even as far back as the 1600s, when the first European settlers arrived in America. On the basis of past and current data, it can also predict what might happen to various habitats in the future.

NATIONAL PARKS ARE ESSENTIAL TO SCIENCE

America's national parks are places where science has profoundly affected the protection and preservation of wildlife habitats. These vast expanses of land, which are run by the federal government and owned by all Americans, are home to a wondrous variety of wildlife species. In the United States there are more than four hundred national parks, which conservation scientist Ryan Valdez refers to as "living laboratories for scientists and resource managers" and "critical hotspots for scientific research and discovery." These parks, says Valdez, have a long history of supporting scientific discoveries. "Their resources, accessibility, unspoiled nature and remarkable geographic distribution make them the greatest collection of study sites a scientist could possibly ask for," says Valdez.

America's first national park, Yellowstone, was established on March 1, 1872, by President Ulysses S. Grant. The massive Yellowstone National Park covers nearly 3,500 square miles (9,065 sq. km). It is mostly in Wyoming and also stretches into parts of Idaho and Montana. The park is home to abundant and diverse wildlife, with sixty-seven species of mammals, nearly three hundred species of birds, sixteen species of fish, five species of amphibians, and six species of reptiles. In the nearly 150 years since Yellowstone was established as a national park, it has provided scientists with a wealth of information about habitats and the creatures that depend on them.

Ryan Valdez, "Why Science Matters for National Parks," National Parks Conservation Association, April 21, 2007. www.npca.org.

The first task for LANDFIRE—and it was a massive one—was to determine how the more than eighteen hundred ecosystems throughout the United States looked and functioned hundreds of years ago. The result was the very first detailed "encyclopedia of ecosystems." Using that, scientists were able to create data sets (collections of related data) that illustrated the current condition of each ecosystem along with its natural condition. "These datasets paint a picture of the entire landscape," says ecologist Randy Swaty. "They are not only beautiful, but allow conservationists to understand what they are dealing with."[13]

LANDFIRE has been extraordinarily useful to scientists who are studying wildlife habitats. It has been used for monitoring the habitats of Rocky Mountain bighorn sheep in Idaho, Oregon, and Washington. It has enabled scientists to monitor habitat conditions along the Appalachian Trail, which stretches more than 2,000 miles (3,219 km) along America's East Coast. It has mapped the potential for wildfire throughout the United States and helped scientists develop plans to restore forests where fires have already occurred.

Another way scientists used LAND-FIRE was to create a map of wild bee habitats in California. The state is one of the top-ranked agricultural areas in the world and leads the nation in agricultural production and exports overall. California supplies 99 percent or more of crops such as almonds, garlic, olives, artichokes, and walnuts. Because bees as pollinators are crucial for crop production, scientists were asked to determine the health of California's bee populations and the habitats that support them. Using LANDFIRE, scientists mapped bee habitats in the state's farm regions and described the conditions that might influence the health of those regions. Scientists hope that this information will help California landowners choose agricultural practices that protect and preserve bee habitats.

WORDS IN CONTEXT

data set

A collection of related data.

Citizen Science

Most scientists do not work alone; they usually collaborate with other scientists doing similar research. In some cases they team up with people who are not professional scientists but are interested in taking part in research. This is at the heart of citizen science, which is also called crowd science. Interested citizens volunteer their time to assist scientists with a wide variety of research projects. These amateur scientists can help in many ways, such as sharing their observations of certain species, taking photos, or finding information on the Internet. "Citizen science is important!" says the Cornell Lab of Ornithology (study of birds). "It's a partnership between the public and professional scientists that can help answer questions scientists couldn't answer on their own."[14]

The Citizen Wildlife Monitoring Project, which is sponsored by the conservation group Conservation Northwest, is among the largest citizen science efforts in North America. Amateur scientist volunteers track and monitor wildlife to assist scientists in the Northwest. In 2016 more than eighty volunteers installed and maintained cameras in twenty-seven different surveying areas in Washington State and in British Columbia in Canada. By examining photos taken by the cameras, the participants detected a number of species, including the gray wolf, mountain lion, fisher (a member of the weasel family), black bear, marten (another relative of the weasel), moose, mule deer, snowshoe hare, porcupine, bobcat, and coyote, among others. "Throughout the year," says Conservation Northwest, "we captured photo evidence of rare wildlife moving in areas where we've never documented them before." The group adds that the Citizen Wildlife Monitoring Project is generating important results for rare and recovering species. "The data our volunteers collect supports state and federal conservation efforts, and with it we'll continue to fight for our native wildlife and help ensure their successful recovery!"[15]

Scientists in other parts of the world are also embarking on wildlife research with assistance from volunteers. In South Africa, for instance, a long-term citizen science study revealed in 2017 that critical forest habitat for birds was seriously threatened by deforestation. South Africa is home to a spectacular variety of birds, including parrots, blue cranes, hawks, African penguins, sunbirds, crowned eagles, and grey louries. These and other South African birds are dependent on forest habitats for survival; they need trees for housing, nesting, protection, and food. But according to the citizen science study, about half of South Africa's forest-dependent bird species are vanishing.

Although only 1 percent of South Africa's landscape is forest, these forests provide a habitat for 14 percent of the country's terrestrial birds. As the study confirmed, when forests are cut down, habitats are fragmented or destroyed, and many species of birds cannot survive. According to ecologist Michael Cherry, wildlife species other than birds may be even more threatened by deforestation. "If birds—perhaps the most mobile of animals—are being negatively affected by forest degradation," says Cherry, "other animal species are likely to be worse affected."[16] On the basis of the study, scientists are evaluating what can be done to better protect avian habitats in South African forests.

Traps That Are Not Really Traps

Citizen science projects are not only for adult volunteers. Many opportunities for involvement in these research projects are available for young people. Children and teens who are interested in science-related projects, including those involving wildlife, can become involved in citizen science efforts. "Citizen science creates opportunities for young people to connect with the natural world, gain scientific skills, and learn key science concepts related to topics such as life cycles, habitats, adaptations, and interrelationships,"[17] says the Cornell Lab of Ornithology. One citizen science program for youth is Nature Navigators, which is for youth in Los Angeles, California, aged nine to twelve. Young people who are involved in Nature Navigators have the chance to participate in different kinds of wildlife research with scientists.

Twelve-year-old Rachel Ann Arias developed a passion for wildlife science through her involvement in the Nature Navigators program. "I think citizen science is a lot of fun," says Rachel Ann. "I enjoy helping scientists and I also enjoy seeing how citizen scientists like me can gather a wide range of observations."[18] What especially intrigued her was learning how to use camera traps. These are cameras that are encased in a secure housing and equipped with sensors that take a picture whenever they sense movement. The name is misleading because camera traps have nothing to do with trapping, as the WWF explains: "While a 'camera trap' might sound menacing, it actually does no harm at all to wildlife. The name is derived from the manner in which it 'captures' wildlife—on film!"[19]

> **WORDS IN CONTEXT**
>
> **camera trap**
>
> A camera encased in a protective housing and equipped with sensors that takes pictures whenever it senses movement.

Wildlife biologist Miguel Ordeñana told Rachel Ann and the other kids about camera traps when he was working with their Nature Navigators group. He taught the young citizen scientists how camera traps worked. He explained the importance of choosing the right location to set up the cameras, the importance of tracking nocturnal species, and other information they needed to know. Rachel Ann yearned for her own camera trap and received one for her birthday. She eagerly began setting it up. On a trip to Yellowstone National Park with her family, she received tips from a biologist. She began following his advice and made some adjustments—and was thrilled with her discoveries. She captured photos of two bobcats together, which is a rare occurrence, since they are solitary animals. Also caught on film was daytime footage of a coyote traveling along the edge of a residential community.

In Venezuela a biologist and a park ranger check the camera trap that they are using to study rare and elusive jaguars. These special cameras are equipped with motion sensors that enable them to capture videos and photos of animals in their natural settings.

And Rachel Ann was excited to see photos of a black bear that her camera trap captured.

Camera traps used at nature reserves in China have helped wildlife scientists learn more about the behavior of giant pandas, which are generally very shy animals. Because of this, little is known about their behavior. From 2010 to 2014 the WWF and the Chinese government collectively managed a wildlife monitoring project. Scientists set up camera traps in twenty-nine Chinese nature reserves that were home to the pandas. The camera traps captured remarkable images and video footage of the giant pandas. "These photos offer a fascinating glimpse into the lives of giant pandas, as well as other animals, which are difficult to see in the wild," says Sybille Klenzendorf, who directs the WWF's species program. "They demonstrate that by saving the iconic giant panda, we secure a vibrant future for other incredible wildlife, wild places and people."[20]

So Many Possibilities

Wildlife habitats are a continued source of interest for scientists. If habitats are not preserved and protected, it could mean the end of the wildlife species that depend on those habitats for food and water, protection, and space to raise their young. No matter where these habitats are, from the rangelands of California to remote jungles in Indonesia, scientists are exploring them using an amazing array of high-tech innovations: drones, artificial intelligence, computer modeling software, and camera traps, just to name a few. Scientists are also able to expand the breadth and depth of their research by working with volunteer citizens who are interested in doing wildlife research. Undoubtedly, even more sophisticated ways of studying wildlife habitats will be developed in the coming years. That will be vital because earth's wild creatures, whose habitats have been lost because of human actions, now need humans to undo the damage.

CHAPTER TWO

Feeding the World, Conserving the Wild

> **"Once a forest is lost to agriculture, it is usually gone forever—along with many of the plants and animals that once lived there."**

—The WWF, which seeks to stop the degradation of the planet's natural environment

World Wildlife Fund, "Overview," 2017. www.worldwildlife.org.

When avid readers hear the name Jack London, they undoubtedly recall the acclaimed author of more than fifty books, including the famous classic *Call of the Wild*. Many people are not aware that London was also one of the first true organic farmers and is considered a pioneer of sustainable farming. In 1905 he bought 130 acres (52.6 ha) of land in Northern California's Sonoma County. He initially viewed the property, which he named Beauty Ranch, as a secluded haven where he could write his books and possibly do a little farming on the side.

It soon became obvious to London that most of the neighboring ranchers were desperately poor and felt hopeless. Based on the condition of their own land, they assured London that his farm was useless for growing anything. He refused to believe that, but after clearing a portion of his land to plant hay, he understood what they meant. For more than forty years the previous landowners, whom London called "our wasteful pioneer farmers,"[21] had nearly ruined the land with old-fashioned farming methods that stripped the soil of nutrients. He was troubled by how carelessly the land had been farmed and was determined to undo the damage. He was not sure how to go about the task since he knew virtually nothing about farming, but he vowed to figure it out.

Healing the Land

London began reading everything he could find about farming techniques. He pored over books, scientific papers, and agricultural journal articles. He also asked for expert advice in letters he wrote to the agricultural departments of the state of California and the University of California. As he continued to build his knowledge about farming, he developed a concept of what he believed would be the ideal farm—one that was sustainable, with farming methods that enriched the land rather than depleting it. "I adopted the policy of taking nothing off the ranch," he wrote in a letter to a friend, adding that he wanted "to leave the land better for my having been [there]."[22] Finally, London felt ready to start putting to work all that he had learned from his research.

No matter what he grew on his farm, London eschewed the use of chemicals and instead recycled manure from his livestock for a natural, organic fertilizer. He grew crops on hillsides using techniques that he had learned in Korea and Japan, where he served as a war correspondent. Known as terrace farming, the practice involved cutting out stair-like terraces to create different levels of growing, which prevented water from washing away the soil. "I had noticed the way the soil was washed down the hillsides by rains and I determined to prevent that," London wrote, "which I did by grading the land, making it over into rolling contours and abrupt terraces."[23] The innovative farming techniques London implemented proved to be successful and productive, with record crop yields—on land that had been deemed worthless.

Energized by his farming success, London expanded the farm by purchasing more land. He began making plans for the future, but his health was poor and continued to grow worse. In 1916 London died at age forty. The farm that he had lovingly nurtured lived on, and today Beauty Ranch is a historic park that is open

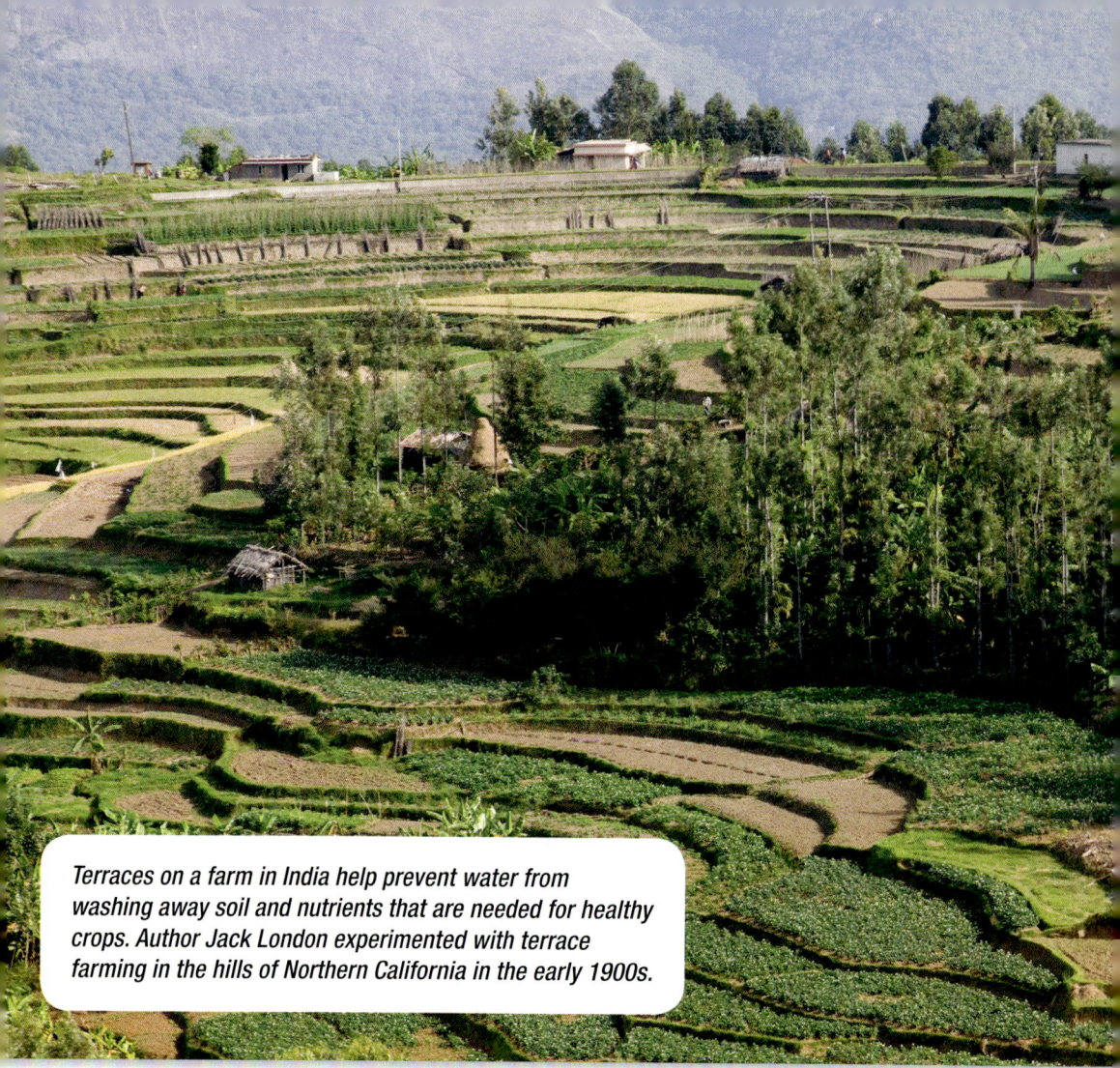

Terraces on a farm in India help prevent water from washing away soil and nutrients that are needed for healthy crops. Author Jack London experimented with terrace farming in the hills of Northern California in the early 1900s.

to visitors. "The world remembers Jack London as a wonderful writer," says author Len Wilcox. "We should also remember him for his pioneering work in sustainability. He helped mold a farm philosophy that builds for the future."[24]

Farming Sustainably, Protecting Habitats

The commitment to take from the land only what will be replaced is at the heart of sustainable agriculture. As with London, people who own and operate sustainable farms have a deep respect for the natural environment. They adhere to the philosophy that land is not something to be used up; rather, it should be continuously replenished. Along with reverence for the environment, people involved in sustainable farming understand the importance of doing everything possible to protect and preserve wildlife habitats—two concepts that are very much intertwined. "When agricultural operations are sustainably managed," says the WWF, "they can preserve and restore critical habitats, help protect watersheds, and improve soil health and water quality."[25]

A farm that is widely acclaimed as a model of sustainability is Davis Ranch, which is located in California's Central Valley. The farm spans thousands of acres, with rice the most prominent crop. A host of other crops—including tomatoes and walnuts—are also grown at Davis Ranch. Yet the family-owned farm is dedicated to much more than growing crops. Its owners are committed to farming sustainably and taking numerous measures to protect wildlife habitat.

One measure Davis Ranch's owners have taken is to plant hedgerows adjacent to rows of crops. Hedgerows are wild shrubs growing closely together to form boundaries, and on Davis Ranch these provide foraging opportunities for Swainson's hawks. Trees for nesting are plentiful around the farm fields, and this has attracted many different species of birds. Environmental Defense Fund (EDF) research associate Scott Sellers visited Davis Ranch and observed, "On the clear blue day you could see and hear birds in every corner of the expansive property."[26] Davis Ranch also has created and preserved habitat for the giant garter snake, as well as built a habitat for monarch butterflies.

The environmental science group Union of Concerned Scientists (UCS) refers to the growing trend of sustainable agriculture as a "transformation" that is taking place on farms throughout the United States. For decades most of the nation's food has been produced using industrial agriculture methods, which involve growing the same crops year after year and using chemical fertilizers and pesticides. "This system is not built to last, because it squanders and degrades the resources that it depends on," says the UCS. "But a growing number of innovative farmers and scientists are taking a different path, moving toward a farming system that is more sustainable—environmentally, economically, and socially."[27] The UCS identifies four major components of sustainable agriculture. These are building and maintaining healthy soil (without depleting it of nutrients); managing water wisely; using practices that avoid air and water pollution; and maintaining biodiversity, meaning a balanced ecosystem in which crops are rotated and plenty of space is allocated for native plants and wildlife habitat.

At Iowa State University in Ames, Iowa, students run their own small sustainable farm. Those who work at the farm grow more than forty different fruits, vegetables, and herbs. Through this experience they learn about all aspects of growing food, from planting, fertilizing, and weeding to harvesting. They also learn to manage a business, since the produce they grow is either sold or donated to residents in need. Heidi Engelhardt, an Iowa State University student who majors in culinary science, says that when she first became involved with the farm, she had no idea how passionate she would feel about the work involved. She enjoyed it so much that she became the farm's outreach coordinator. Engelhardt says that students in her major typically want to work in kitchens and also in big cities. "And that is important," she says, "but it's also important to have that farming aspect. And I think I'm very lucky to have discovered that."[28]

Beneficial for the Land and Wildlife

Farmers whose operations are truly sustainable use a number of innovative practices, one of which is no-till farming. Tilling, in conventional agriculture, involves using a plow outfitted with a mechanical device (a tiller) that digs into the soil, turns it over, and breaks up the clumps. In the process, soil is loosened, weeds are chopped up, and residue from the previous crop is removed. A growing number of farmers are using no-till farming, which is better for the environment. Rather than digging up the ground after a harvest, farmers allow the residue (such as corn stalks and leaves) to remain on the field during the off-season.

When this organic matter is left on a field, it improves soil quality, better retains water, and reduces erosion. Also, once the harvest has been completed, the untilled field naturally becomes a habitat for wildlife. "No-till relies on natural processes to break down residue from the previous crop,"[29] says Brian Scott, a farmer from northwestern Indiana who uses the no-till approach on his farm. Scott adds that when it is time to plant, he uses machinery that sweeps the residue out of the way so seeds can be placed in furrows but does not create any trenches in the soil.

Another farmer who believes strongly in no-till farming is Carl R. Mattson, who owns the sprawling Mattson Farms in Chester, Montana. He is a staunch supporter of sustainable farming and was one of the first farmers in Montana to adopt the no-till method. Mattson switched to the practice in 1993 primarily for soil conservation but learned over time that no-till farming also helps

A farmer in Maryland tills his field in preparation for the next crops. Some farmers have begun using no-till farming; they say it improves soil quality, does a better job of retaining water, and reduces erosion.

well. "The emphatic 'BOB-white' call of quail used to be widespread, but now is hard to find," says Dan Small, who is a field ecologist with Washington College in Chestertown. "There don't seem to be as many fireflies or butterflies as when we were kids and there certainly aren't the same number of ducks as there were in our grandfather's youth."[32]

These changes to the Eastern Shore, says Small, have resulted from a combination of growing population and the rise of intensive farming. But as troubling as the situation may be, it can be turned around. A program known as the Natural Lands Project, which Small coordinates, seeks to restore the rural landscape and rebuild wildlife habitat in partnership with local farmers. The farmers sign a ten-year contract. The cost of seed and planting is covered, and for their participation they receive a small incentive payment, which helps offset the loss of crop production. Small provides some examples of how beneficial the program will be for wildlife:

> Native warm season grass plantings replace marginal crop land, improving wildlife habitat and the water quality downstream at the same time. Wet and poorly drained sections of fields can be converted to wetlands which attract wintering waterfowl, like the American Black Duck. A wildflower "pollinator patch" installed close to the farm house can create a beautiful vista that also hosts native bees and supplies the Monarch Butterfly with the milkweed it needs to reproduce.[33]

An important part of the Natural Lands Project is the construction of buffer strips, which are strips of land 100 feet (30.5 m) wide that farmers plant with grasses and wildflowers. These buffers absorb excess chemicals, nutrients, and sediments used in farming (known as agricultural runoff), and this prevents the substances from entering waterways and causing environmental damage. The buffers also provide habitat for many types of wildlife, including bobwhite quail and other species of birds, as well as small mammals. And because of how they filter runoff, buffers make water habitats cleaner for rockfish, oysters, and blue crabs.

Progressive Farmers

One farmer who participates in the Natural Lands Project is Brennan Starkey, who owns a farm on the Sassafras River in Galena, Maryland. Of his total land, 550 acres (222.6 ha) are natural areas that are made up of woods and wetlands. "It provides excellent habitat for all manner of wildlife," says Starkey. He has been involved in various conservation programs for more than twenty years and built buffer strips throughout the farm in 1989. He became part of the Natural Lands Project soon after the program was implemented and says the reason it interested him was because "it was a natural extension of what we were already doing."[34]

Of special interest to Starkey was being part of the effort to reestablish populations of bobwhite quail in the region. He has not seen the birds around his farm for at least the past five years, and he is eager for them to return. His farm is teeming with plenty of other wildlife, however. "We have a very healthy population of wild bees, butterflies, woodpeckers, herons, and eagles,"[35] he says. Also on the Starkey farm are plenty of rabbits and foxes, as well as wetland critters such as turtles, otters, and crayfish.

Another farmer who is involved with the Natural Lands Project is Bob Ingersoll, who owns a farm in Chestertown. His participation is somewhat unusual, since he has enrolled his entire 60 acres (24.3 ha) in the program. Fields that have grown hay for more than fifteen years are now covered in native grasses and wildflowers like blue mistflowers and chicory flowers. This drastically changed landscape has resulted in some remarkable differences on Ingersoll's farm. "We have a lot more small birds here than we did any year that I can remember, because there's something there for them to eat," he says. "And butterflies! I've never seen so many butterflies."[36] As word spreads about the benefits of the Natural Lands Project, Small and his colleagues are hopeful that many other farmers will want to participate.

Habitat Exchanges

Another type of incentive program for farmers to help save wildlife is known as the habitat exchange. Under this program, which was developed by the EDF, landowners agree to protect, restore, conserve, and in some cases create wildlife habitat on their land. "Farmers do a great job of growing stuff," says the EDF's Eric Holst, "and wildlife relies on habitat that can also be grown or tended to by farmers or ranchers."[37]

According to the EDF, habitat exchanges are either in progress or are being developed for a variety of wildlife species. One species that is a high priority is the monarch butterfly, whose population is in severe decline. According to the EDF, in the past two decades the population of monarchs has plummeted, and the butterfly is now dangerously close to extinction. This is largely due to disappearing habitat—specifically, a wild plant known as milkweed, which monarchs need for laying their eggs and breeding. In the past milkweed plants grew abundantly in many areas of the United States. For a number of reasons, primarily the widespread use of chemical weed killers (herbicides) by farming operations, milkweed is fast disappearing—and when it is gone, monarchs will no longer be able to survive. Farmers involved in habitat exchange programs can help save butterflies by planting milkweed along roadsides instead of converting the areas to cropland. "Since farmers and ranchers manage much of the habitat appropriate for milkweed," says the EDF, "they are in a perfect position to restore and enhance this vital habitat."[38]

Another high priority for the EDF is protecting and restoring the habitat of the greater sage grouse, a bird that is native to western rangelands. In order to survive and thrive, these birds need large expanses of healthy sagebrush grasslands as well

A monarch caterpillar feeds on milkweed. Farmers who have taken part in habitat exchange programs have planted milkweed and other native plants along farm roads to provide badly needed habitat for endangered wildlife such as the monarch butterfly.

as access to water. At the start of the twentieth century, populations of the greater sage grouse topped 20 million. Today, says the US Fish and Wildlife Service, only an estimated 200,000 to 500,000 of the iconic birds remain in the western United States. This decline has occurred largely because oil, gas, and other

FEAR VERSUS SCIENTIFIC EVIDENCE

In recent years some of America's biggest growers of vegetables and salad greens have been concerned about their crops being contaminated by disease-causing bacteria. Due to what investigators reported after a deadly 2006 outbreak of E. coli bacteria in bagged spinach, wild animals were assumed to be the culprits. Because of that, farmers began taking steps to keep their fields completely separate from wildlife habitats. They cut down forest areas adjacent to farm fields, cleared stream banks of grasses and other vegetation, and surrounded their fields with wide strips of bare ground. Environmentalists criticized these practices, saying that the habitat destruction was rooted in fear rather than scientific evidence. In 2015 Nature Conservancy scientist Daniel Karp set out to conduct his own investigation.

Karp and some of his colleagues analyzed thousands of test results from dozens of farms that grew produce. They found that vegetables grown near wildlife habitats were no more likely to be contaminated than produce grown in farms that separated fields from habitats. "In fact, you see no relationship," says Karp. "You do not see that farms that are near habitat have any elevated levels of these pathogens." He and his colleagues also found that in some farms that cleared away wildlife habitat, contamination with E. coli became even more common. So not only was keeping the habitats separate from farm fields not helping, says Karp, "it in fact looked like it was making food less safe."

Quoted in Dan Charles, "Don't Fear the Wild Animals, Researchers Tell Salad-Makers," NPR, August 11, 2015. www.npr.org.

development have destroyed or degraded habitats. Farmers and ranchers who participate in habitat exchanges to help save the greater sage grouse can take a number of steps. For instance, they can protect the best sagebrush habitats from development and can control the expansion of fast-spreading pinyon-juniper trees and invasive plants that encroach on sagebrush habitats. They can also restore sagebrush on degraded lands and more carefully manage livestock grazing to protect habitats.

Worth Saving

Farmers throughout the United States are committed to agricultural practices that are sustainable, respectful of the environment, and protective of wildlife habitat. Prevalence is growing of no-till farming and other innovative, environmentally sound practices. A variety of programs offer farmers incentives to take part of their land out of crop production and turn it into habitat so species that have disappeared might once again return. By participating in habitat exchange programs, farmers are helping save monarch butterflies, greater sage grouse, and other species whose populations have dramatically declined. As these and other efforts continue in the future, perhaps there will come a time when there is no longer a need for an endangered species list.

CHAPTER THREE

Conservation-Minded Development

> **"The good news is that we can save most of these species, but we have to pay attention and leave some habitat intact; we can't convert the entire surface of the Earth to farm[land] or cities and remain unscathed."**

—Joel Sartore, a National Geographic photographer and founder of the Photo Ark project

Quoted in Mary Bowerman, "Half the World's Species Could Go Extinct and You're Part of the Problem," *USA Today*, May 19, 2017. www.usatoday.com.

JFK International Airport in New York City is one of the busiest airports in the world. Originally known as Idlewild Airport, the sprawling facility covers nearly 5,000 acres (2,023 ha) of land—but it was not always land. In the early twentieth century, the coastal lagoon Jamaica Bay and its wetlands and salt marshes covered much of the area. In order for construction on the new airport to begin, about 4,500 acres (1821 ha) of wetlands had to be filled in with earthen material. Back then, these swampy areas were not believed to be important. Scientists did not yet know that wetlands serve as habitats for innumerable species of wildlife, help improve water quality, and perform other vital functions. They were dismissed as useless obstacles that could only have value if they were drained and filled to accommodate development. So in the spring of 1942, much of Jamaica Bay's wetlands were filled in and the airport was built on top of them.

Many years passed before scientists learned about the immense value of wetlands, and they regretted that an irreplaceable ecosystem had been destroyed at Jamaica Bay. When a new runway was proposed in 1968, environmental groups successfully defeated the project because it would have required even more wetland destruction. In the 1970s the US Congress passed environmental legislation that afforded protection for America's wetlands under federal law. Still, development around Jamaica Bay has resulted in the loss of nearly 90 percent of its original wetlands.

Birds, Butterflies, and Trespassing Turtles

The ecosystems that were lost when the wetlands were destroyed are gone forever. But the value of wetlands is now widely known, and today Jamaica Bay Park is a wildlife refuge administered by the National Park Service. The sprawling refuge covers 18,000 acres (7284 ha) made up of wetlands, salt marshes, and numerous islands, as well as two freshwater ponds, meadowlands, and wooded areas. With more than 330 different types of birds sighted there, the park is a haven for bird-watchers. At least sixty species of butterflies can be found in the refuge, along with an array of reptiles, amphibians, and small mammals such as rabbits, squirrels, raccoons, opossums, and muskrats.

One type of reptile that makes its home in Jamaica Bay's salt marshes is a turtle known as the diamondback terrapin. Named for the diamond-shaped markings on its top shell, the terrapin spends nearly all its time in the brackish waters of the marsh. But from June through mid-July of each year, after mating season, the female terrapins leave the marsh and go hunting for a sandy place in which to nest and lay their eggs. That is when things get interesting at the airport, because in their quest to reach sandy soil, the turtles must make their way across one of the runways. "The original airport planners never could have imagined that all the sandy fill

> **WORDS IN CONTEXT**
>
> **brackish**
>
> Slightly salty, such as when river water mixes with seawater.

The Jamaica Bay Wildlife Refuge, within view of New York City, offers a place of serenity for people and wildlife. Airport construction and other development destroyed much of the natural wetlands. The remainder has been preserved as habitat that is now teeming with diverse wildlife.

they put down would one day become the perfect nesting habitat for terrapins,"[39] says wildlife biologist Laura Francoeur.

This annual terrapin crossing is a familiar and expected event for Francoeur and other wildlife professionals who have been rescuing turtles from the JFK runway for years. Whenever one is spotted, flights are delayed until the turtle is removed from the runway. "Anything can be a hazard to aircraft, even turtles,"[40] says Francoeur. Once the creatures are captured, they are measured, their shells are marked, and they are electronically tagged for identification. Then they are taken away and released somewhere they can safely nest.

The Port Authority of New York & New Jersey, which manages the airport property, installed plastic barriers to keep the turtles off the runway. Although it helped cut down on the trespassing terrapins, the barriers have not stopped their migration completely. During June and July 2016, more than five hundred females were captured, processed, and released into the wild.

A Necessary Balance

A busy airport in a major city is but one example of how human development has crowded and squeezed wildlife and habitats. Land is continuously in high demand for housing, office buildings, strip malls, parking lots, recreation facilities, and industrial sites, as well as for energy production and road building. As land is cleared for these and other types of infrastructure development, fragmentation, degradation, or complete destruction of wildlife habitat is the inevitable result. The WWF writes: "A road cuts through pristine rainforest to give a community access to the city. A dam creates a reservoir to provide freshwater to a growing town. A platform that is miles from the shoreline gives access to oil reserves deep below the ocean floor. These are all examples of infrastructure— physical structures that provide the underpinnings for modern society."[41] Although infrastructure development is a crucial part of a growing population and makes modern life and convenience possible, without careful planning it has the potential to devastate the natural world.

> **WORDS IN CONTEXT**
>
> **infrastructure**
>
> Physical structures that enable a society to grow and prosper, including roads, railways, and water and gas pipelines.

A high priority for wildlife scientists is conceiving ways to lessen the impact of human development on wildlife habitats. There are many situations when environmentally sound practices can be part of early development planning, rather than having to cope with mistakes later. "Environmental concerns are not always considered during the design, planning and construction of infrastructure projects,"[42] says the WWF. Conservation scientists from the WWF and other environmental groups work with governments, industry, and other leaders to encourage that sustainability be considered in the early planning phases of any kind of development. This could result in minimal environmental impact and protection of delicate habitat that could easily be destroyed without careful planning in advance.

Growing Dilemmas in Florida

The concept of building in green practices sooner rather than later when a development is planned is widely embraced by environmental scientists. This is especially important in areas of high population growth where new development is a certainty. Florida, for example, currently has about 20 million residents. According to a 2016 study, the population is projected to soar to 33.7 million by 2070—with at least one-third of the state covered in roads, houses, and other buildings. If this development is not well thought out in advance, Florida's magnificent array of wildlife could be decimated as its habitat is slowly destroyed. Elizabeth Fleming, who is with the environmental group Defenders of Wildlife, offers this scenario:

> Picture a stretch of iconic Florida habitat. Pines tower over prairie grasses swaying in the wind between clumps of saw palmetto. A red-cockaded woodpecker flits between the trees, while a gopher tortoise digs diligently beneath the earth, and Florida panthers wander through in search of food, water, or a safe place to rear their young. Then plans for a new building or a residential community are announced—right on that very spot. All that habitat, relied on by so much wildlife, could be simply gone. Now picture the same scenario playing out hundreds of times across an entire state.[43]

According to Fleming, whose work focuses on conserving wildlife habitat for numerous species, the scenario describes what is happening in Florida today. As the population continues to grow, it will trigger even more development. Even when Defenders of Wildlife or another environmental group is able to prevent a damaging project from being completed, Fleming says another one pops up to take its place. "A new residential development in a fragile ecosystem here, a road widening through panther habitat there," she says. "Trying to stave off damage to the habitats that Florida's imperiled wildlife most desperately need seems at times like a game of 'whack-a-mole' with incredibly high stakes and no end in sight."[44]

A POTENTIAL CATASTROPHE FOR WILDLIFE

During the 2016 presidential campaign, Donald Trump talked a great deal about a border wall between the United States and Mexico. That border spans nearly 2,000 miles (3,219 km), so construction would take years and cost billions of dollars. With all the hurdles involved, no one knows if the wall will ever be built. But one thing is known: Such a wall would be catastrophic for wildlife. The border that winds along the southern edge of Texas, New Mexico, Arizona, and California serves as habitat for hundreds of wildlife species, and the wall would cut through the habitat and fragment or destroy it. The wall would also overlap four wildlife refuges that are home to a variety of animals that would no longer be able to migrate in order to hunt, mate, and find water. "It will choke off life from both sides," says wildlife biologist Jeff Corwin.

One animal that is threatened by the wall is the jaguar, the largest cat in the Western Hemisphere. During the nineteenth and early twentieth centuries, jaguars roamed freely throughout the American Southwest. Today wildlife officials know of only two adult male jaguars in the United States. If their population is ever going to grow, the cats will need to mate with female jaguars from Mexico. That is already a challenging feat because of the distance they must travel. If their efforts are met with a three-story-high concrete wall, it will mean the end of wild jaguars in the United States.

Quoted in Daniella Silva and Suzanne Gamboa, "Trump's Border Wall 'Catastrophic' for Environment, Endangered Species: Activists," NBC News, April 22, 2017. www.nbcnews.com.

Like others in her profession, Fleming is convinced there is a better way to go about addressing Florida's development needs. The ideal solution, she says, is bringing together landowners, residential and commercial developers, wildlife advocates, and conservation experts, with the goal of getting everyone to agree on a plan for an entire landscape. Fleming explains what is needed:

A plan where those who are fighting to keep wildlife and their habitats on the map actually get to influence where development projects go, and where they don't. Instead of battling each project on its own and risking a loss, we could make certain that the most important habitats are declared "off limits," protecting them from not one or two but ALL development projects planned for decades to come.[45]

This already exists, says Fleming, in a program called the Habitat Conservation Plan, which Defenders of Wildlife is working to implement in Collier County in southwest Florida.

The Habitat Conservation Plan is intended to protect sixteen different species indigenous to Florida that are listed under the ESA. One of these is the severely endangered Florida panther.

The habitat of the endangered Florida panther (pictured) is being squeezed by development. These cats once roamed freely throughout the southeastern United States. Nowadays they are often killed by cars traveling on roads that crisscross their habitat.

Although these majestic cats once roamed freely throughout the southeastern United States, today they are restricted to less than 5 percent of their original range. If the panther population grows, which wildlife scientists hope it will, the cats will need much more room than they have now. That will mean moving north, where there is more habitat suitable for them: swamps, forests, and prairies where panthers can live, breed, and raise their young.

There is a problem, however, when the panthers start migrating north—roads that they must cross, which are a deadly hazard. "In that direction lies a landscape criss-crossed with miles of roads," says Fleming. "And as far too many of these endangered panthers have learned over the years, they are no match for a speeding car."[46] Fleming's hope is that programs like the Habitat Conservation Plan can help prevent panthers and other wildlife from continuing to lose critical habitat as human development crowds them even more than it is today.

A Company That Cares

Along with wildlife scientists and other environmental professionals, many businesses are concerned about endangered wildlife and the loss of habitat. This is true of the technology giant Google, a company that is widely known for being environmentally responsible, devoted to sustainability, and committed to using 100 percent renewable energy. Google's headquarters is a huge office complex in Mountain View, California. One hundred fifty years ago, the site was covered in grasslands, wildflower-filled meadows, and wetlands. Also, there were sprawling groves of willow trees and abundant oaks. Later, a large chunk of the land was cleared for farming, and it remained that way for decades. Then in the 1990s it became the site of an office park. In 2003, when Google moved into the building, the company began working with teams of professionals to restore the landscape to its natural state as much as possible.

In one project the landscape group worked closely with the City of Mountain View to expand a small willow grove called the Charleston Retention Basin. This expansion was an effort to re-create the massive groves that once grew throughout the area.

"One missing element of the landscape today are these willow groves—these large, wooded wetland areas that were associated with high groundwater, and provided a lot of food resources throughout the year for a lot of species,"[47] says Robin Grossinger, an environmental scientist who worked with Google on the landscaping design. In the past, she says, the willow groves helped wildlife survive during periods of drought. Expanding the groves will be beneficial to wildlife during future droughts.

Google is also working with its landscape group on what is called a "re-oaking" project. This is intended to bring back valley oak trees that were once abundant on the land, and it will hopefully attract wildlife species that depend on the trees. Google management authorized the removal of 134 parking spaces in company lots to make room for habitat expansion. As of February 2017 a total of 50 acres (20.2 ha) of the Google campus have been converted to more native landscaping, with more being planned for the future.

Roads Cut Through Habitat

Of all the threats faced by wildlife and all the ways habitats are fragmented or destroyed, roads and highways are among the worst problems. Yet the reality is that society cannot function without roads. They provide vital and necessary functions, from allowing people access to employment, education, health care, recreation—and other people—to transporting goods from manufacturers to consumers. "Roads and railways are necessary to move goods and people across distances," says the WWF, "but they have long-lasting effects on the landscapes they cut through."[48]

In several Asian countries, proposed roads could severely endanger habitat for tigers, and the big cats are already struggling to survive. According to Jon Miceler of the WWF's Asia Programs, 97 percent of the tiger population has disappeared from the wild in the past century. The tigers that exist today inhabit only around 7 percent of their original range. In Laos, Cambodia, and Vietnam, the tiger population has declined to the point that the animals are considered extinct; a few may exist, but there are no breeding pairs that can reproduce. There are still tigers in

REDESIGNING WITH NATURE

When considering examples of sustainable development, few people would include golf courses on their list. Although beautiful, these sprawling expanses of lush green turf are often viewed as excessive users of water and chemicals like fertilizers and weed killers. But according to the environmental nonprofit organization Audubon International, up to 15 percent of golf courses in the United States and Canada are members of environmental programs. The facilities have committed to principles of conserving water, scaling back on the amount of manicured turf, naturalizing areas not used for play, and protecting wildlife habitat around the courses.

At one of these courses, located in Vero Beach, Florida, the superintendent planted more than eight hundred native plant species and removed invasive species. Also, he stopped the practice of having lake-bank grasses mowed and allowed them to grow naturally. This resulted in buffer zones around ponds that absorbed chemical runoff, which improved habitat for fish and created habitat for birds and butterflies. Similar steps were taken at a golf course in Stone Mountain, Georgia. Grounds director Anthony Williams implemented a natural mosquito-control system by having two dozen bat boxes constructed—a single bat eats thousands of mosquitoes each night. Williams added thirty-six nest boxes for bluebirds and stopped mowing 14 acres (5.7 ha) of the course to restore habitat. "What we've learned," he says, "is that everything we do as an operation has an impact on wildlife and the environment around us."

Quoted in Lisa D. Mickey, "Golf Courses Taking Key Steps to Become Good Neighbors," Audubon International, January 8, 2016. www.auduboninternational.org.

India, Nepal, Indonesia, Russia, and China, but they are seriously threatened. Miceler estimates that the total tiger population in the wild is fewer than four thousand. Because of growth in Asia, he says, about 6,800 miles (10,944 km) of infrastructure (roads, railway, high-tension wires, water, and gas pipelines) will be needed. "And," says Miceler, "virtually all those plans will cut through what is prime tiger habitat."[49]

Like other environmental scientists, Miceler believes it is possible to accommodate the needs of a growing population and economy while also protecting wildlife habitat. For instance, sophisticated computer mapping software can show ecosystems like watersheds and forests, as well as other types of habitats. By putting this incredible science to work, says Miceler, progress can still continue, but development will be done in the right way. "We're not saying don't build roads," he says. "But there's a green way to do it. And that's what we're advocating."[50]

Wild animals throughout the United States are continuously threatened by infrastructure expansion. In Southern California, for instance, scientists are trying to solve the problem of rapidly shrinking mountain lion habitat. Like tiger habitat in Asia, mountain lion habitat is being crowded out by development; most of the available habitat for these big cats is sandwiched between the major cities of Los Angeles and San Diego, where an estimated 20 million people live. Research has shown that as Southern California's population continues to grow, the mountain lions' chances of survival will continue to fall.

Wildlife Crossings

To increase wildlife's chances of survival in the Canadian province of Alberta, environmental scientists worked with transportation officials to come up with a creative solution: adapt roads to accommodate wildlife. When the Trans-Canada Highway was built, it cut up wildlife habitats and also created a large barrier to animals' movement. The solution was to construct overpasses and underpasses, known as wildlife crossings, to span the highway. These structures are designed and built to help animals cross the road safely, which is always a serious risk when habitats have been cut off by roads or highways.

Along the Trans-Canada Highway in Alberta's Banff National Park, there are now forty-four wildlife crossings: six overpasses and thirty-eight underpasses. These structures have also been built along highways in two other Canadian national parks, both of which are in the province of British Columbia. Officials estimate that this solution has resulted in an 80 percent decline in car-animal collisions. It has also allowed tens of thousands of animals, including deer, elk, coyotes, wolves, black bears, cougars, and grizzly bears, to cross the highway safely. Environmental scientist

Alberta transportation officials have created wildlife crossings—animal overpasses (pictured) and underpasses—along the Trans-Canada Highway. Scientists say this has greatly reduced the number of car-animal collisions on the highway.

Trevor Kinley says that installing the wildlife crossing structures has benefited humans as well as wildlife. "We've reduced those collisions so that means fewer animals being killed," he says. "It means greater safety for the public and, in particular having those underpasses there, we've also maintained passage for those animals throughout the landscape."[51]

The Solar Energy Challenge

When people consider the reasons for wildlife habitat loss, what comes to mind are likely the most obvious and widespread causes, such as road building or clearing land for residential or business development. But another serious threat to habitat is solar energy—specifically, the installation of large solar farms built in remote regions. This presents a huge challenge, because solar energy is clean energy and completely renewable, meaning that unlike fossil fuels, it will never be used up. Thus, it has immense potential to provide electrical power to people in many areas of the world, including the United States. Large solar farms generate electricity using thousands, perhaps even millions, of photovoltaic panels, which convert sunlight directly into electricity. Once it has been generated, the energy can be piped long distances to residents and businesses. But in order for such a vast number of panels to be installed, vast amounts of wildlife habitat is destroyed. Defenders of Wildlife president Rodger Schlickeisen writes:

> Building a single major solar facility in the California desert can require thousands of acres of biologically-fragile land—land that supports a wide range of sensitive and imperiled species (including the desert tortoise, desert bighorn sheep, and Mohave ground squirrel) and unique habitats—to be cleared and leveled. The sheer size and scope of these projects is difficult to comprehend.[52]

Schlickeisen and other environmental professionals are absolutely in favor of solar energy and other types of renewable energy. But in the same way that roads, office parks, shopping malls, or any other type of development needs to be carefully planned in advance, large solar installations must be as well. Their environmental impacts, including the effects on wildlife habitat, need to be anticipated and thoroughly evaluated at a very early stage.

Wind Farms

The same is true of large wind installations; their potential impact on wildlife habitat must be considered early in the planning process. Like solar power, energy from the wind is clean and renewable, and many environmental scientists say its immense potential has barely been tapped. But wind energy is generated by massive turbines, many of which stand 300 feet (91.4 m) to 400 feet (122 m) high. These towering structures with their huge spinning blades carry a severe and deadly risk for birds. According to the National Audubon Society, wind turbines kill as many as 328,000 birds each year in North America. Many deterrents have been developed to scare birds away from the turbines, including brightly colored blades, bright lights, different designs of blades, and several other concepts, but none has proved to be effective in decreasing bird deaths.

Because wind power has tremendous potential as a green energy source for the future, environmental scientists widely tout its expansion. But most agree that wind farms must be carefully planned and installed in areas that are not known as primary migration pathways or bird stopover points. One example of a wind farm that was installed without such planning is the Altamont Pass Wind Farm in Northern California. The facility was built during the 1960s in the midst of a major avian migration route. As a result of its placement, tens of thousands of golden eagles, burrowing owls, red-tailed hawks, and other types of birds, as well as untold numbers of bats, have been killed. In 2015 the owner of the wind farm announced that the oldest and most dangerous of the turbines would be shut down and replaced.

A Choice

In any advanced society, development is inevitable as well as essential. A part of population growth is growing infrastructure, including roads and highways, housing, commercial and industrial facilities, and energy generation. Yet wildlife, which has already been harmed in so many ways by human actions, now depends on humans for its very survival. If habitat preservation is not considered a high priority when any type of development is planned, humans can blame no one but themselves when earth's wildlife continues to disappear.

CHAPTER FOUR

How Climate Change Threatens Habitats

> **❝Climate change is altering key habitat elements that are critical to wildlife's survival and putting natural resources in jeopardy.❞**
>
> —National Wildlife Federation, America's largest conservation organization
>
> National Wildlife Federation, "Effects on Wildlife and Habitat." www.nwf.org.

Since the earth has existed, it has experienced natural fluctuations in climate: periods of cooling, followed by periods of warming, and then back to periods of cooling. There is strong evidence, from record high temperatures in numerous cities to massive ice melting in the Arctic, that the planet is again in a warming period. Most scientists emphasize, however, that what is happening now is anything but natural. They warn that the planet is heating up more rapidly than at any time in history.

Some of the most compelling signs of rapid climate change are the effects on wildlife habitats. "Climate change is altering key habitat elements that are critical to wildlife's survival and putting natural resources in jeopardy," says the National Wildlife Federation. Melting ice in the Arctic Circle; warming oceans, lakes, and rivers; and severe droughts are all signs of how climate change is altering natural habitats. Human populations may increasingly experience difficulties as a result of these changes, but they can adjust to changing conditions more easily than animals. As the National Wildlife Federation explains, "Species may not be able to adapt to this rapid climate change or to move fast enough to more suitable areas as their current areas become less suitable for them."[53]

An Unnaturally Warming World

Environmental groups such as the National Wildlife Federation, along with most of the world's scientists, say that the unnatural warming is a result of human actions. Not everyone agrees with this—but the number of doubters has been shrinking over the years as evidence of climate change becomes more difficult to refute. According to the National Aeronautics and Space Administration (NASA), 97 percent of climate scientists now agree that climate-warming trends over the past hundred years "are very likely due to human activities, and most of the leading scientific organizations worldwide have issued public statements endorsing this position."[54] Whatever the cause, no one can deny that the earth is heating up, and this is creating serious problems for wildlife habitats throughout the world.

The human activity that is widely believed to be the culprit of the fast-warming climate is the burning of fossil fuels: coal, oil, and natural gas. These fuels all have a high concentration of carbon. When they are burned, the combustion produces massive amounts of a colorless, odorless gas called carbon dioxide (CO_2), and this gas is emitted into the atmosphere. This occurs in a number of different ways. For instance, CO_2 is created when coal is burned in power plants to generate electricity. According to the US Energy Information Administration, 35 percent of the total CO_2 emissions in the United States during 2016 were from coal-fired power plants. CO_2 is also produced when people burn gasoline or diesel fuel in their vehicles; when rain forests are cut down and burned for agriculture; and when factories manufacture metals, chemicals, plastics, and minerals, generating CO_2 as a by-product.

CO_2 is a powerful heat-trapping gas, so named because when it is in the atmosphere, it traps and holds heat from the sun. It is also called a greenhouse gas since its heat-trapping capability

Motorists make slow progress on a typical Los Angeles freeway. Gasoline- and diesel-powered vehicles emit carbon dioxide, which scientists around the world say is a major contributor to climate change.

resembles how a greenhouse holds the sun's heat to keep plants warm all year long. Two other gases, water vapor and methane, also have heat-trapping capability. Together, these greenhouse gases linger in the atmosphere to regulate earth's temperature like a natural thermostat, which keeps the climate in balance. Without greenhouse gases the planet would be too cold for humans and other living things to survive. If too high a concentration of these gases builds up in the atmosphere, earth would grow too hot to support life. Although both of these are extreme scenarios, climate scientists are alarmed at what is currently happening to the climate—and what it could mean for earth's inhabitants.

Convincing Evidence

One area of the world where signs of a rapidly warming climate are virtually everywhere is the Arctic Circle. A large body of research has shown that the entire planet is warming, but the Arctic is heating up at least twice as fast as the rest of the world. "It has been a record year so far for global temperatures, but the record high temperatures in the Arctic over the past six months have been even more extreme,"[55] says NASA sea ice scientist Walt Meier. Such unusually high temperatures in the Arctic have led to widespread melting of sea ice, glaciers, ice sheets, and ice shelves. Normally, ice cover in the Arctic Ocean declines by about 50 percent during the summer, although some of the ice never melts. But because of rapid Arctic warming, there is less ice cover than usual. Scientists offer the dire prediction that by the mid-2020s most of the Arctic Ocean will be completely ice free during the summertime.

In April 2017 scientists from the University of Kansas published photographic evidence of global warming's effects on earth's polar ice formations. They collected photos taken many years ago and compared them with current photos of the exact same regions. The old photos showed what glaciers used to look like in the Arctic (specifically, Greenland) and Antarctica, which is the world's southernmost polar region. The comparison between old and new was shocking for the scientists, because the current photos clearly showed a vast reduction in ice. "We have unretouched photographic evidence of glaciers melting all around the globe," says ecologist Gregory Baker, who led the study. "That includes the ice sheets of Greenland and Antarctica—they're reduced in size." Baker emphasizes that these findings were not the result of computer models or satellite images. "These are simply photos, some taken up to 100 years ago, and my co-authors went back and reacquired photos at many of these locations," he says. "So it's just straightforward proof of large-scale ice loss around the globe."[56]

Arctic Crisis

The rapid, widespread melting of Arctic ice has proved to be devastating for many types of wildlife. One animal that is especially threatened by the shrinking ice is the polar bear, which lives only in the Arctic. The polar bear is the only species of bear that is a marine mammal, meaning one that completely depends on the ocean for food and habitat. These enormous bears—males can weigh nearly 1,000 pounds (454 kg)—spend most of their time on Arctic sea ice, where they hunt for food. Their diet consists almost exclusively of calorie-rich ringed seals. In areas where there is no sea ice during the summer months, like Hudson Bay, Canada, polar bears live on land until the water freezes over again in the

The effects of climate change are most stark in the Arctic, where rapidly melting ice threatens the survival of polar bears. As ice melts, polar bears must swim across larger stretches of open water in search of food.

fall. "While on land during the summer," says the National Wildlife Federation, "these bears eat little or nothing."[57] When the bitterly cold winter returns and the bay is once again frozen, the bears can venture back onto the ice and hunt for seals.

Research has shown that over the past two decades, the ice-free period in Hudson Bay has increased by an average of twenty days. What that means for polar bears is that their time to hunt for food has declined by nearly three weeks. As a result, says the National Wildlife Federation, the average weight of polar bears has dropped by 15 percent, which in turn has caused reproduction rates to decline. Another problem caused by melting Arctic ice is that the remaining ice keeps moving farther and farther from shore, and the distance between sheets of floating ice (known as ice floes) continues to widen. Polar bears typically swim about 30 miles (48.3km) at a time. Because of rapid ice melt, however, there are now larger stretches of open water that the creatures must swim across in order to reach ice. This creates a hazardous situation for them and has led to a number of drownings.

In 2011 scientists at the US Geological Survey (USGS) used a tracking device to record the journey of a female polar bear in the Beaufort Sea, which is north of Alaska. Accompanied by her yearling cub, the female swam more than 400 miles (643.7km). For nine days the bear swam continuously, trying to reach an ice floe where she could hunt for food. "We are in awe that an animal that spends most of its time on the surface of sea ice could swim constantly for so long in water so cold," says USGS zoologist George M. Durner. "It is truly an amazing feat." Yet the unbelievably long swim came at a very high cost for the bear. She lost an estimated 22 percent of her body fat, and along the way her cub drowned. "It was simply more energetically costly for the yearling than the adult to make this long distance swim,"[58] says Durner. He adds that as the planet continues to warm, the stretches of open water will keep widening.

The slow, steady loss of polar bear habitat represents a serious threat to the survival of these animals. According to Durner, this complete dependency on sea ice for survival potentially makes the polar bear "one of the most at-risk large mammals to climate change."[59] Many other scientists and environmental organizations agree with this dismal prediction. The USGS projects that two-thirds of earth's polar bears will disappear by the year 2050.

Wildlife in Peril

Along with polar bears, countless other wildlife species are also threatened by melting Arctic ice, although not necessarily in the same way. As massive ice shelves and glaciers melt, an incredible amount of water pours into the ocean, which in turn causes sea levels to rise. Sea levels are also affected by rising ocean temperatures. As seawater warms, it expands and takes up more space, which causes even more of a rise in sea level. Scientists warn that these changes will lead to severe flooding of coastal areas throughout the world—and devastating consequences for humans and wildlife.

The sea turtle is one species that is threatened by coastal flooding. The reptiles use both marine and land habitats during their life cycles, and a rise in sea level could destroy their nesting beaches. According to the Sea Turtle Conservancy, the memories of sea turtles are "imprinted" with a map of the sandy beach where they once hatched. In an ancient nesting ritual, female turtles return to the same site over and over again to nest and deposit their own eggs. "With melting polar ice caps and rising sea levels," the Sea Turtle Conservancy writes, "these beaches are beginning to disappear."[60] Another risk to sea turtles is their sensitivity to ocean water temperatures. As ocean water grows warmer, it could negatively affect their food resources. Coral reefs, which are an important food source for sea turtles and many other marine creatures, are already dying because of warming ocean

WILDLIFE ESCAPE ROUTES

As earth's climate continues to heat up, wildlife will either have to adapt to hotter temperatures or flee to new, cooler habitats farther north. The problem is that the forests, deserts, mountains, parks, and fields where wildlife species now live have been fragmented by human development: sprawling cities, large agriculture operations, and roads—and these are only a few of the hurdles animals would encounter if they try to migrate. Getting through such a maze of human development would likely be impossible for wildlife, so scientists have proposed a solution: the creation of migration corridors, which could serve as escape routes for migrating wildlife.

These would not be corridors in the literal sense; the idea of clearly defined paths for animals to travel on as they head north is unrealistic. Rather, these corridors could be created through the restoration of forests and other natural areas in order to form a connection between current habitats and probable destination sites. According to Georgia Tech ecologist Jenny McGuire, migration corridors are something that land managers need to be thinking about right now. She says that wildlife species need "little plant and animal highways, paths that make it easier to move and disperse over the landscape."

Quoted in Simone M. Scully, "Habitat Corridors Could Help Save Wildlife from Climate Change," Business Insider, June 13, 2016. https://amp.businessinsider.com.

water temperatures. A major new study that appeared in the journal *Nature* in March 2017, for instance, described catastrophic bleaching in Australia's Great Barrier Reef. Bleaching caused by spikes in ocean water temperature kills coral reefs, transforming the normally brilliant colors into a sickly white.

Seabirds are also threatened because of rising sea levels. Following a twenty-year study of large wading birds called Eurasian oystercatchers, researchers from Australia concluded that the birds are not able to survive coastal flooding. This, say the researchers, is the reason for declining populations of oystercatchers. "Sea level rise and more frequent flooding are major drivers of this steep decline in coastal birds,"[61] says scientist Liam Bailey, who led the research. Because Eurasian oystercatchers live in an area where flooding is becoming more common, Bailey says this poses a threat to the survival of these shorebirds. The study also found no evidence that the birds have tried to escape flooding by increasing the height of their nests, even among birds that lost nests during a flood. This may be due to the presence of predators or unsuitable nesting vegetation. Whatever the reason, it further emphasizes that Eurasian oystercatchers are in danger of becoming extinct.

Research has also shown that populations of coastal marsh birds along the East Coast of the United States are in sharp decline. One of these is the saltmarsh sparrow, an orange-faced bird that lives in the salt marshes of the Atlantic and upper Gulf Coasts. According to Bailey, these members of the sparrow family are struggling to survive because of rising sea levels and increasing flooding. He believes they could be driven to extinction within the next twenty years. "Like the Eurasian oystercatcher, this species does not appear to be adapting to the changing tidal conditions," says Bailey. A similar study of coastal birds in Europe showed strong declines in populations there as well. "Our work," says Bailey, "is part of a growing amount of research that shows the vulnerability of coastal bird species. These species may need additional conservation focus in the future."[62]

A World Without Bees?

Scientists have made similarly bleak discoveries about the ability of bees to survive in a warming world. Bee populations have already plummeted due to habitat loss, widespread use of pesticides in farming, and other factors. Climate change creates even more problems for bees. They cannot survive extreme temperatures, and prolonged heat waves can dry up their food sources. As a result of stressors that affect bees, compounded by a warming climate, bee populations have been declining by as much as 30 percent per year. Environmental groups that study bees say that there were twice as many honeybee colonies in 1959 as there are today. And honeybees are not the only bees that are threatened.

According to a 2015 study of bumblebees by researchers from Canada, as temperatures steadily rise, massive numbers of bees are being killed off. But the researchers found that unlike many other species that respond to a warming climate by migrating northward toward the polar regions, bumblebees are not moving. Biologist Jeremy Kerr, who led the study, says that he and the other researchers were shocked that the bees had not moved. "We thought bumblebees would do that,"[63] he says. One reason Kerr and his colleagues assumed the bees would move is because of the behavior of butterflies, which migrate north when southern climates are not habitable. Even though it seems like bees could easily do the same, the scientists are puzzled about why this is not happening. It could be that the habitat farther north is not suitable for them, although that is only speculation.

Bumblebees (pictured) perform a vital function by pollinating many agricultural crops and other plants, including wildflowers. Scientific studies show that the warming global climate is killing enormous numbers of bees.

Kerr and the team of researchers who conducted the study, along with other scientists who touted its importance, emphasize that further research is imperative. Bumblebees perform a vital function by pollinating many agricultural crops as well as wildflowers, and it would be disastrous if they became extinct. "It is very concerning that they are struggling to adapt to climate change around the world,"[64] says Canadian scientist Nigel Raine.

A Continuing Quest for Knowledge

Researchers throughout the world continue to explore the effects of climate change on all kinds of species, from bumblebees and

RELOCATING WILDLIFE

Human intervention to save species from extinction is nothing new. The California condor population, for example, had declined to just twenty-three birds in 1982. Five years later all wild condors were caught and placed in captive breeding programs. Since 1992, when the birds were released back into the wild, the population has grown to 410. Similar efforts have saved rare species like the Arabian oryx (a type of antelope), golden lion tamarin (a small gold-colored monkey), and Vancouver Island marmot (a large squirrel), as well as species of fox, bumblebee, mink, and tortoise.

Some scientists believe the time has come to do even more. German-born scientist Axel Moehrenschlager is one of these scientists. "We are in a situation of emerging threats due to climate change," he says, adding that if species are not more actively managed, "we will lose them." Moehrenschlager advocates moving threatened wildlife from one area to another, a process known as translocation. There are risks involved with translocation. For instance, relocated species could overpopulate a new area, thereby threatening the survival of native species. Moehrenschlager says it is important to consider the potential risks and plan for them in advance. "Success is not guaranteed," he says, "but the alternative of not acting is guaranteed—and that is extinction."

Quoted in Jessica Aldred, "More than 1,000 Species Have Been Moved Due to Human Impact," *Guardian* (Manchester), April 20, 2016. www.theguardian.com.

shore birds to polar bears and sea turtles. With each new discovery and each piece of compelling evidence, the necessity of continuing this research grows more pressing. Scientists say it is imperative for them to better understand the impact of a warming climate on individual wildlife species. According to ecologist Erik Beever, it is the responsibility of scientists to learn as much as they can about how climate change affects wildlife and habitats. "Because," he says, "if we don't understand how and why species are being affected, we don't know what to try to do with climate [adaptation] management or conservation."[65]

Because the Arctic is heating up twice as fast as the rest of the world, it is a high priority for climate change research. Scientists at the University of Calgary in Canada have been studying narwhals, which are a type of whale with a large protruding "tusk" (actually an enlarged tooth). This tusklike tooth is so pronounced that narwhals have been called "unicorns of the sea." During late summer, the Canadian Arctic is mostly ice-free, and narwhals swim into deep-water inlets along Baffin Island in the Canadian territory of Nunavut, where researchers are able to study them.

One of these researchers is Sandra Black, who is trying to determine how changes in the Arctic might be affecting narwhals. "There is this overarching question about what the impacts are in the Arctic," says Black. "The question is, will the narwhal be resilient to the changes that have and will continue to occur?"[66] Black's research is ongoing, and she has not arrived at any definitive conclusions about narwhals' ability to cope with climate change. But previous research has shown that warming ocean waters will kill off fish that narwhals depend on for food, which would present a serious threat.

Frightening Findings

Some climate change research confirms what scientists already suspected, while other studies have produced disturbing new findings. This was the case with a 2017 study by Australian researchers, who found that the negative impacts of climate change on wildlife have been massively underestimated. According to this research, at least seven hundred bird and mammal species have been affected by climate change, including many already on the endangered species list. Lead researcher James Watson notes that most climate change research has focused on effects fifty or even one hundred years in the future. The new study differs in that it shows that climate change is already a major threat to hundreds of species. Watson says it is a "scientific problem in that we are not thinking about climate change as a present-day problem, we're always forecasting into the future." He adds, "When you look at the evidence, there is a massive amount of impact right now."[67]

A staggering array of wildlife, including animals on every continent, was found to be threatened by climate change. Those identified included elephants, eastern gorillas, snow leopards, and a wide variety of birds. Particularly hard hit by the effects of a warming climate were animals with highly specialized diets and those that live in high altitudes, like the snow leopards, which live in the mountains of central Asia. But the researchers found that even animals with a wide range of diet are suffering from massive declines. "We have seriously underestimated the effects of climate change on the most well-known groups," says Watson. For other species such as reptiles, amphibians, and fish, he continues, "the story is going to be much, much worse in terms of what we think the threat is from climate change already."[68] Watson emphasizes that it is vital for climate change to be addressed as a significant threat to wildlife now, rather than something that could happen years from now.

An Uncertain Future

Earth's climate is getting hotter, and most scientists agree that this is not a product of nature. The rapidly warming planet includes not only the temperature of the land but also the oceans, which are also becoming warmer. This is wreaking havoc with all kinds of wildlife, and as the warming continues, the effects on wildlife will likely grow more severe. How many of these species will be able to survive such drastic changes is unknown, but there is strong evidence that many will not. Scientists fear numerous species will become extinct as their habitats degrade and disappear. Researchers continue to aggressively study climate change to monitor its effects on wildlife habitats and to investigate possible ways of mitigating the damage. At this point, what is unknown is far greater than what is known.

SOURCE NOTES

Introduction: Saving Habitats to Save Wildlife

1. National Wildlife Federation, "Habitat Loss." www.nwf.org.
2. World Wildlife Fund, *Living Planet Report 2016: Risk and Resilience in a New Era*. Gland, Switzerland: WWF International, 2016. https://c402277.ssl.cf1.rackcdn.com.
3. Endangered Species Coalition, "Protecting the Endangered Species Act," 2015. www.endangered.org.

Chapter One: Science to the Rescue

4. World Wildlife Fund, "Impact of Habitat Loss on Species," 2017. wwf.panda.org.
5. Quoted in Elizabeth Soumya, "Eyes in the Sky: The Incredible Technology Helping Save Asia's Wildlife," Love Nature, October 20, 2016. http://community.lovenature.com.
6. Serge Wich and Lian Pin Koh, "From the Forest: Aerial Flights Survey Orangutans—the Conservation Drone Project," Orangutan Conservancy, September 14, 2012. www.orangutan.com.
7. Wich and Koh, "From the Forest."
8. Quoted in Kate Baggaley, "Drones Are Setting Their Sights on Wildlife," *Popular Science*, February 20, 2017. www.popsci.com.
9. Quoted in Olivia Bailey, "Conservation Drone Reveals Uncharted Seagrass Habitat in Cambodia," Phys.org, May 26, 2016. https://phys.org.
10. Quoted in John R. Platt, "Drones Uncover Illegal Logging in Critical Monarch Butterfly Reserve," TakePart, June 22, 2016. www.takepart.com.
11. Quoted in Nature Conservancy, "Terra-i: A Cool Tool for Deforestation," 2017. www.nature.org.
12. Quoted in Nature Conservancy, "Terra-i."
13. Randy Swaty and Jeannie Patton, "My LANDFIRE Decade: The Amazing Story of a Critical Tool for US Restoration," *Cool*

Green Science (blog), Nature Conservancy, May 15, 2015. https://blog.nature.org.

14. Cornell Lab of Ornithology, "Citizen Science for Educators," 2017. www.birdsleuth.org.

15. Conservation Northwest, "Citizen Wildlife Monitoring Project Makes New Discoveries," January 6, 2017. www.conservationnw.org.

16. Quoted in *Daily Dispatch* (East London, South Africa), "Bird Species in Deadly Danger," February 10, 2017. www.pressreader.com.

17. Cornell Lab of Ornithology, "Citizen Science for Educators."

18. Quoted in *Nature in L.A. Blog*, Nature at NHMLA, "Teen Empowerment Through Citizen Science," February 21, 2017. https://nhm.org.

19. World Wildlife Fund, "Camera Traps," 2017. www.worldwildlife.org.

20. Quoted in World Wildlife Fund, "How Camera Traps Help Panda Conservation," August 25, 2016. www.worldwildlife.org.

Chapter Two: Feeding the World, Conserving the Wild

21. Quoted in Rebecca Sweet, "Jack London? One of California's First Sustainable Farmers? Who Knew!!," *Gossip in the Garden* (blog), Harmony in the Garden, 2017. http://harmonyinthegarden.com.

22. Quoted in Charles Levine and Mike Benziger, "London's Greatest Tome: A Legacy of Sustainable Farming," *Sonoma Index-Tribune* (Sonoma County, CA), May 26, 2016. www.sonomanews.com.

23. Quoted in Jack London State Historic Park, "Jack London's Terraces." http://jacklondonpark.com.

24. Len Wilcox, "Jack London: The Father of Sustainable Farming," Real Western View, July 31, 2015. https://therealwesternview.com.

25. World Wildlife Fund, "Sustainable Agriculture," 2017. www.worldwildlife.org.

26. Scott Sellers, "Birds, Snakes and Butterflies: Farming for More than Crops and Cash," *Growing Returns* (blog), Environmental Defense Fund, July 27, 2016. http://blogs.edf.org.

27. Union of Concerned Scientists, "What Is Sustainable Agriculture?" www.ucsusa.org.

28. Quoted in Amy Mayer, "A Student-Run Farm Cultivates Passion for Sustainable Agriculture," NPR, June 7, 2016. www.npr.org.

29. Brian Scott, "What Is No-Till?," *The Farmer's Life* (blog), April 26, 2013. http://thefarmerslife.com.

30. Carl R. Mattson, "Written Statement for the Record: Strengthening Conservation Through the 2012 Farm Bill," US Senate testimony, US Senate Committee on Agriculture, Nutrition, & Forestry, February 28, 2012. www.agriculture.senate.gov.

31. Mattson, "Written Statement for the Record."

32. Dan Small, "Natural Lands Project," Washington College Center for Environment and Society. www.washcoll.edu.

33. Small, "Natural Lands Project."

34. Brennan Starkey, e-mail interview with author, June 4, 2017.

35. Starkey, interview.

36. Quoted in Chesapeake Bay Program, "Restoration Spotlight: Striking a Balance Between Farming and Wildlife Habitat," October 31, 2016. www.chesapeakebay.net.

37. Quoted in Carrie Arnold, "New Schemes Pay You to Save Species—but Will They Work?," *Smithsonian*, July 13, 2016. www.smithsonianmag.com.

38. Environmental Defense Fund, "Habitat Exchanges: How Do They Work?," 2017. www.edf.org.

Chapter Three: Conservation-Minded Development

39. Quoted in Jessica Hershman, "JFK International Airport: Terrapin Adventures on Runway 4L," Port Authority of New York & New Jersey, July 21, 2016. https://portfolio.panynj.gov.

40. Quoted in *U.S. News & World Report*, "Kennedy Airport Take-offs Disrupted by Turtle Nesting Ritual," July 15, 2016. www.usnews.com.

41. World Wildlife Fund, "Threats: Infrastructure," 2017. www .worldwildlife.org.

42. World Wildlife Fund, "Threats."

43. Elizabeth Fleming, "What the Collier County HCP Could Mean for Florida Wildlife," Defenders of Wildlife, June 20, 2016. www.defendersblog.org.

44. Fleming, "What the Collier County HCP Could Mean for Florida Wildlife."

45. Fleming, "What the Collier County HCP Could Mean for Florida Wildlife."

46. Fleming, "What the Collier County HCP Could Mean for Florida Wildlife."

47. Quoted in Adele Peters, "How Google Is Restoring Wildlife Habitats in the Middle of Silicon Valley Office Parks," *Fast Company*, February 3, 2017. www.fastcompany.com.

48. World Wildlife Fund, "Threats."

49. Quoted in Ann M. Simmons, "New Asian Roads Could Mean End of the Road for Tigers, Wildlife Official Says," *Los Angeles Times*, April 13, 2017. www.latimes.com.

50. Quoted in Simmons, "New Asian Roads Could Mean End of the Road for Tigers, Wildlife Official Says."

51. Quoted in Colette Derworiz, "How Do the Animals Cross the Road in Banff National Park?," *Calgary (AB) Herald*, May 2, 2016. http://calgaryherald.com.

52. Rodger Schlickeisen, "Making Renewable Energy Wildlife Friendly," Defenders of Wildlife. www.defenders.org.

Chapter Four: How Climate Change Threatens Habitats

53. National Wildlife Federation, "Effects on Wildlife and Habitat." www.nwf.org.

54. National Aeronautics and Space Administration, "Climate Change: How Do We Know?," June 1, 2017. https://climate .nasa.gov.

55. Quoted in National Aeronautics and Space Administration, "2016 Climate Trends Continue to Break Records," July 19, 2016. www.nasa.gov.

56. Quoted in Brendan M. Lynch, "In New Paper, Scientists Explain Climate Change Using Before/After Photographic Evidence," University of Kansas News, April 18, 2017. https://news.ku.edu.

57. Quoted in National Wildlife Federation, "Global Warming and Polar Bears." www.nwf.org.

58. Quoted in Ella Davies, "Polar Bear's Epic Nine Day Swim in Search of Sea Ice," BBC, January 25, 2011. http://news.bbc.co.uk.

59. Quoted in Davies, "Polar Bear's Epic Nine Day Swim in Search of Sea Ice."

60. Sea Turtle Conservancy, "Threats to Sea Turtles." https://conserveturtles.org.

61. Quoted in Phys.org, "Sea Level Rise May Drive Coastal Nesting Birds to Extinction," June 1, 2017. https://phys.org.

62. Quoted in Phys.org, "Sea Level Rise May Drive Coastal Nesting Birds to Extinction."

63. Quoted in Adam Vaughan, "Climate Change Causing Bumblebee Habitat Loss, Say Scientists," *Guardian* (Manchester), July 9, 2015. www.theguardian.com.

64. Quoted in Vaughan, "Climate Change Causing Bumblebee Habitat Loss, Say Scientists."

65. Quoted in Elizabeth Harball, "Climate Change Proves a Survival Experiment for Wildlife," *Scientific American*, February 7, 2014. www.scientificamerican.com.

66. Quoted in Phys.org, "What Does the Arctic Tell Us About Climate Change?," May 11, 2017. https://phys.org.

67. Quoted in Scott Waldman, "Climate Change Has Already Harmed Almost Half of All Mammals," *Scientific American*, February 15, 2017. www.scientificamerican.com.

68. Quoted in Waldman, "Climate Change Has Already Harmed Almost Half of All Mammals."

FIND OUT MORE

Books

Lynn E. Barber, *Birds in Trouble*. College Station: Texas A&M University Press, 2016.

Mary Ellen Hannibal, *Citizen Scientist: Searching for Heroes and Hope in an Age of Extinction*. New York: Experiment, 2016.

Robert Llewellyn and Joan Maloof, *The Living Forest*. Portland, OR: Timber, 2017.

Brenda Peterson, *Wolf Nation: The Life, Death, and Return of Wild American Wolves*. Boston: Da Capo, 2017.

Lori Robinson and Janie Chodosh, *Wild Lives: Leading Conservationists on the Animals and the Planet They Love*. New York: Skyhorse, 2017.

Internet Sources

Andy Coghlan, "Europe Is Rapidly Losing Its Biodiversity and Wildlife Habitats," *New Scientist*, May 18, 2015. www.newscientist.com/article/dn27543-europe-is-rapidly-losing-its-biodiversity-and-wildlife-habitats.

Darryl Fears, "These Creatures Faced Extinction. The Endangered Species Act Saved Them," *Washington Post*, March 11, 2017. www.washingtonpost.com/amphtml/news/animalia/wp/2017/03/11/eight-animals-saved-from-extinction-by-the-endangered-species-act.

Andrew Mach, "Animal 'Selfies' Show How Protecting Wildlife Habitats Is Paying Off," *PBS NewsHour*, January 30, 2016. www.pbs.org/newshour/rundown/animal-selfies-show-how-protecting-wildlife-habitats-is-paying-off.

Matt Miller, "10 Innovations That Are Changing Conservation," *Cool Green Science* (blog), Nature Conservancy, June 2, 2016. http://blog.nature.org/science/2016/06/02/10-innovations-changing-conservation.

Elizabeth Soumya, "Eyes in the Sky: The Incredible Technology Helping Save Asia's Wildlife," Love Nature, October 20, 2016. http://community.lovenature.com/wild/eyes-in-the-sky-the-in credible-technology-helping-save-asias-wildlife.

Ryan Valdez, "Why Science Matters for National Parks," National Parks Conservation Association, April 21, 2017. www.npca.org /articles/1523-why-science-matters-for-national-parks#sm.0000 bmagj8190mfo2pgwxisag20cn.

Todd Wilkinson, "Threatened Species Are Thriving in Yellowstone. Now What?," *National Geographic*, May 2016. www.national geographic.com/magazine/2016/05/yellowstone-national-parks -wildlife-restoration.

Websites

Bird Sleuth (www.birdsleuth.org). A project of the Cornell University Lab of Ornithology, Birth Sleuth is a site especially designed for young people who want to learn more about birds. Separate sections (such as Bird Identification, Citizen Science, Bird Biology, and School Gardens) each offer a wide variety of interesting information about birds and their habitats.

Habitats, BBC (www.bbc.co.uk/nature/habitats). This information-packed website offers an extensive array of photos, facts, and interesting details about wildlife habitats. One section focuses on terrestrial (land) habitats, while the others focus on freshwater habitats and marine (ocean) habitats.

Habitats, World Wildlife Fund (www.worldwildlife.org/habitats). Those seeking to learn more about earth's wildlife habitats will find a wealth of information on this site, which covers forest habitats, ocean habitats, and habitats in freshwater, grasslands, wetlands, deserts, mountains, and polar regions.

US Environmental Protection Agency (https://www.epa.gov). This federal government website offers plenty of information about environmental topics (such as pesticides, waste and clean up, and green living) and about environmental laws and regulations.

US Fish & Wildlife Service (www.fws.gov/endangered). This federal government website offers plenty of information about threatened and endangered plants and animals.

INDEX

PICTURE CREDITS

ABOUT THE AUTHOR

Peggy J. Parks holds a bachelor of science degree from Aquinas College in Grand Rapids, Michigan, where she graduated magna cum laude. An author who has written nearly 150 books for young people on a wide variety of topics, Parks lives in Muskegon, Michigan, a town she says inspires her writing because of its location on the shores of beautiful Lake Michigan.